Real Estate

Going From Novice to Full-Time Real Estate Pro

Table of Contents

Introduction 5

Chapter 1: Real Estate Investment Basics 6

Chapter 2: Becoming a Real Estate Agent 15

Chapter 3: House Flipping Basics 22

Chapter 4: Rental Property Basics 28

Chapter 5: REIT Basics 37

Chapter 6: Property Wholesaling Basics 42

Chapter 7: What Buyers Expect from a Realtor 49

Conclusion 51

The following Book is produced below with the goal of providing information that is as accurate and reliable as possible. Regardless, purchasing this Book can be seen as consent to the fact that both the publisher and the author of this book are in no way experts on the topics discussed within and that any recommendations or suggestions that are made herein are for entertainment purposes only. Professionals should be consulted as needed prior to undertaking any of the action endorsed herein.

This declaration is deemed fair and valid by both the American Bar Association and the Committee of Publishers Association and is legally binding throughout the United States.

Furthermore, the transmission, duplication or reproduction of any of the following work including specific information will be considered an illegal act irrespective of if it is done electronically or in print. This extends to creating a secondary or tertiary copy of the work or a recorded copy and is only allowed with express written consent from the Publisher. All additional right reserved.

The information in the following pages is broadly considered to be a truthful and accurate account of facts and as such any inattention, use or misuse of the information in question by the reader will render any resulting actions solely under their purview. There are no scenarios in which the publisher or the original author of this work can be in any fashion deemed liable for any hardship or damages that may befall them after undertaking information described herein.

Additionally, the information in the following pages is intended only for informational purposes and should thus be thought of as universal. As befitting its nature, it is presented without assurance regarding its prolonged validity or interim quality. Trademarks that are mentioned are done without written consent and can in no way be considered an endorsement from the trademark holder.

Introduction

Congratulations on acquiring *Real Estate: Going from Novice to Full-Time Real Estate Pro*. I would like to take this time to thank you for doing so. The information contained in this presentation will enlighten you on the path you will be taking as a real estate investor, agent, or other related position.

The ensuing chapters will discuss the basics of the real estate world for you as a beginner who is not sure of which segment of real estate you would like to enter.

The knowledge you gain from learning the basics of investment in real estate and how to become an agent will enable you to place yourself in a position to continue the process.

House flipping has become advertised and popular over the years which you might consider as your chosen path. Rental properties also hold an active portion of the industry. Understanding the basics of REIT as well as property wholesaling will enlighten the path towards your decision.

Many skills will be required from you if you choose real estate for your career. This guideline will take you from the very basic essentials to a successful agent, investor, or any other specialty fields you choose to follow.

There are plenty of books on this subject on the market, thanks again for choosing this one! Every effort was made to guarantee it is chock full of as much useful information as possible; please enjoy!

Chapter 1:
Real Estate Investment Basics

You will be putting your hard earned dollars to work when you make real estate investments, so you can increase your earnings in years to come. Of course, your return or profit needs to be sufficient to cover all of the risks involved owning property. You need to consider the investment costs such as regular maintenance, insurance, taxes to be paid, and utilities. Even if the property is not occupied, it has to be maintained to remain a good investment.

Ways to Make Money

Plan 1: Cash Flow Income: You can invest in properties whereas tenants will pay you for the use of the property for a specified time. Cash flow income can be collected from office buildings, apartment buildings, rental homes, car washes, or well-operated storage facilities.

Plan 2: Real Estate Depreciation or Appreciation: It is a risky challenge once property values increase because of the fluctuation in landholdings. The property around residential homes can change quickly if a major convenience center (similar to Wal-Mart) moves into the neighborhood. If you are seeking investments, this could hurt your chances of locating reasonably priced property.

Plan 3: Real Estate Linked Income: Real estate brokers fall into this category as a specialist who receives salaries/commissions by selling and buying property. Some management companies may also receive daily percentages of the rentals for managing the business or property.

As an example, if you purchase a motel, the management company could receive a percentage from handling the daily routines—for instance—hiring the staff or operating the call center as well as other related activities required at the establishment.

Plan 4: Real Estate Auxiliary Investment Income: This type of income is considered a 'business within a business' investment. For example, you can invest in vending machines located in laundry facilities or office buildings, and receive profits from the operation of them.

Guidelines for Success

Since you are just starting out, it is difficult to focus on what you need to do first to begin your road to a successful career. These are a few tips to guide you through each phase:

Phase 1: Be Determined: This is a huge asset—determination—because real estate investment is a lifelong pursuit which can engulf your financial future. Investments will not get you rich in a hurry, and you will surely make some mistakes along the way. The secret is to learn from the wrong turns and get back on the path with clarity, and know you can accomplish your goals.

Phase 2: Educate Yourself: It is essential to understand the lingo of what the seasoned real estate investors are speaking about in general conversations. Get acquainted with your associates and learn some of the 'ropes' that can only be learned by experience. You need to read all of the current information you can find on investments in the area where you want to acquire real estate.

Phase 3: Be Creative: Change your thought patterns from 'I think I can' to 'I will be successful.' By simply changing the way you look at investment or any part of your life can make you successful.

Phase 4: Become Math Conscious: Keeping accurate records is essential, but first, you have to keep up with all of the expenses. Check all of the figures of properties you are interested in, and be sure they are competitive with the location. You have to make sure you have a solid business deal, and that includes you understanding the basics of the spreadsheet. Put your deal on paper with dollars and cents (sense too), so you can see where your money is going. Real estate is a number game that you have to stay on top of at all times for success.

Phase 5: Business is Business: Stay organized as you would with any job you have, even if it is your daily life. You need to continue with efficiency and remember it not a hobby, and you as a business owner has to hold high standards and do your best.

Phase 6: Get Experience: It is important to keep your regular job if you decide to invest in real estate. With an economy that is already in stress, you have to be careful of how you spend your money.

Phase 7: Present a Map: You need to make a clear path concerning which direction you want to take with your investments. How many successful investors do you know that did not have a plan to become wealthy?

Phase 8: Small Investments are Acceptable: It is acceptable to start small with your investments. It can begin with purchasing your home. You could also decide to go with a partnership later. That is what is good about investment opportunities; it is up to you. It will be your business.

Phase 9: Write a Catchy Listing: If you are a listing agent, you need to learn how to write a description that will make your property all but jump off of the page and snatch a buyer. If you play on the emotional card, you will most likely get his/her attention. For example, have a happy couple standing in front of the home with a newborn baby and a sold sign in the background with your name on it; it doesn't get better than that!

Investment Tips

Location is Essential: You have always heard the old saying of location matters, and it is very true when purchasing investment property. Before you go into debt; you need to be sure it is in a favorable neighborhood. Ultimately, search for a home or other building that is in need of repair.

You can build equity when you take the 'worst' home (needs work) and mix it with the 'best' locale. In other words, you take a home in need of repair, and sell the property ready to go with a remodeling job. This is called flipping (discussed in a later chapter).

Tip 1: Search for Wholesale Property Locations: You will be searching for tract of land (with or without a home) that has been listed at a huge discount. All that is required is to check all of the numbers to see if a profit can be acquired from the purchase. This is called the return on investment or ROI. You can also check on **Auction.com** or similiar sites.

Tip 2: Figure the Tax Advantages: It is a fact that the government wants business owners (private investors) to house the people in this country. If enough is not provided, it will be up to the government to provide the housing. With that said, investors can receive a tax deduction in the form of a depreciation write-off if there is a building/home on the property.

You need to check for clarification with your tax agent for the specifics, but in essence it is approximately 27 years for residential buildings, and commercial buildings are 39 ½ years. Since investors fall under a business category, the IRS allows 'ordinary and necessary' deductions such as insurance, maintenance, mortage interest, and similiar expenses.

Tip 3: Review Your Credit Report: To become a successful real estate person, you have to have good credit. It is essential to obtain a copy of the credit report which can also be accomplished on the Internet. You can check the scores free at websites such as Quizzle or Credit Karma. If you discover any issues, whether they are right or wrong, you need to take care of the problem right away.

Most lenders in today's market require a minimum of 700 FICO (Fair Issac Co.) for those applying for the purchase of real estate investment property. The three major companies are Equifax, Experian, and Trans Union. Another factor to be considered is the total debt-to-monthly-income ratio which should be low. The ratios can be improved if you lower the outstanding car loans or debt.

When you are in a position to apply for a loan at the bank; you need to have your credit records available. You must show you have either cleared the debt, made arrangements to clear it, or let your loan officer know it was a mistake. It is advisable to clear or lower the credit card balances in case you need them for future necessities.

Tip 4: Apply the 1% Rule: You should receive a minimum of 1% of the payment price monthly if you rent out the property to tenants. As an example, if the purchase price is $250,000; you should receive $2,500 each month to receive a good ROI. This is a deciding factor whether the property is worth your investment.

Tip 5: Investigate Realtors, Banks, and Mortgage Brokers: Begin your investigation at your current financial institution where you might discover better rates. It is common for first time investors as well as many others to finance its properties. You need to find a company that is reputable and has affordable rates.

Maintain an Online Presence

With today's fast-paced society, communication through the Internet is essential. These are a few things you can do to expand your online marketing efforts:

Consideration 1: Start a Blog

Capturing an audience can be acieved if you choose a topic of interest to blog about to an online reader. For example, you could write an article about your experiences thus far on your journey to becoming an investor, agent, or other similiar position.

You will be amazed how much information can be gathered with the assistance of other people in your situation. Make your blog so effective that you will have a great 'word-of-mouth' type of advertisement. Your site will be the first viewed site by many possible clients or co-workers.

You can write about current market trends, local events, real estate basics, or any topic of interest. Include your personal touches and experience as an additional attraction to the site. Your name will be passed with each share.

Place a video on your blog and add a captivating scene to be clicked that will surely go viral. People are curious by nature; you will be remembered when the like or share button is clicked.

Consideration 2: Real Estate Community Pages

All you need is access to the Internet and a Facebook account to start your own page. You can also go to this link for more information: (*https://knowhownonprofit.org/how-to/how-to-set-up-a-facebook-presence-for-your-organisation-guide*).

Using a community page will allow you to learn more about your community and allow you to share your information to attract the visitors to the site. Once you have their attention supplying them with great information about local attractions, community history, and the neighborhoods in general; you can bet they will notice your investments which are for sale.

Consideration 3: Apply Social Media

Social media is more than just Facebook; it includes Google+, Twitter, Pinterest, and LinkedIn. Each of these outlets provide you with the resources necessary to get your information on the web quickly. The only requirement is that you remain active on the content pages. You have to keep your viewers interested.

You can add 'like' buttons on the page so you can get the prospective clients information. By replying, you keep his/her attention and will socially bring that person back to your site.

However, like most steps in real estate, it is a trial and error process. Remain informative and helpful with various types of suggestions by participation.

Engage with conversations with new home purchasers or use some of your interior design pictures from your property on Pinterest. Your comments could lead one of those new homeowners to a new client. You never know!

Consideration 4: Learn SEO Basics

The Internet can be your best friend if you know how to work the search engine optimization or SEO. If you are a beginner, this is a system used to focus on improving the traffic on your site and increase the awareness in the search engine.

By choosing specficic phrases/keywords and terms to describe your property, you will generate traffic to the website. Once they are on you site, you have to be sure it is full of information that lead the client to your page. Once again, Google is your friend on the pursuit of setting up the SEO to your benefit.

Consideration 5: Locate the Content

It is sometimes difficult to find new content to keep larger audiences coming back to your page. Your community page and blog are great starter projects but you will need to have so much additional content. If you just don't have the time to search for the information, you can go to sites such as *Bundlr*, *Storify*, and *Scoot.it*, for various sources.

You can focus on your audience, while you share the information gathered from the additional platforms. Once again, you have to search for what works best for your individual ideas and needs.

Chapter 2:
Becoming a Real Estate Agent

To become an agent takes patience and time. One of the most important steps to consider as a real estate agent is having a backup source of income. Plan for about six months or more that may lapse before you receive a commission. These are just a few of the essential steps you must take before you can be considered ready to assume the position:

Step 1: Enroll in a pre-licensing course. Each state has specific requirements before you can take the real estate licensing examination. You need to have training from a certified facility to learn the terminology you will need to use such as 'encumbrance' or 'escrow.' You will also learn the legal characteristics of the industry in real estate and how to calculate or determine property values.

Go online to your state's real estate commission to locate the list of recognized institutions where you can attend and a list of the requirements. Decide whether you want to be in a lecture hall setting or take the course online. It depends on which location you feel the most focused.

Step 2: Take the Exam. Typically, exams are separated into two sections; one for the state-specific laws, and the other for general and federal real estate laws and principles. You can go online to the state's real estate commission's website to register for the licensing exam.

The contents of each test are generally 60 to 100 of open-ended questions. You can brush up on your math skills with some sample questions online. You may also need a calculator to answer questions such as the calculation of prorated taxes on a piece of property. If you don't have a calculator, you can usually find one using the Internet.

The good part is that you can attempt the exam for up to two years—as frequently as you wish. However, after two years, you will be required to take the pre-licensing course again.

Step 3: Activate your Privileges: The excitement is astounding because you just completed your testing for your real estate license. Congratulations are in order since you have not joined a worthwhile vital profession. The biggest question now is where to begin, but you will have to make many tough decisions before you are an established realtor.

Go to the website for the state's real estate commission. Check the site for activation fees.

Pay a membership fee to the local multiple listing services (MLS). You must have access to this structure to list the properties. The site will provide you with listings in advance, before they are released to the open market, and also allow you to see the market trends and tax information for the property. Once again, check your state for the fees.

Step 4: Join the National Association of Realtors (NAR). You must be a supporter/member of the NAR if you want to become a qualified realtor. The organization has numerous benefits which can include educational courses at a discounted rate, and it will allow you to access to the marketing data essential for your job as a successful realtor. With the card in your possession with the term "Realtor" listed will add to your trustworthiness.

Step 5: Connect with a Brokerage Firm: You will be directed by an overseeing broker for training to ensure you remain ethical and adhere to all legal steps as a real estate sales person. As time passes, you can take over the broker role, but you need some experience in the field before you can apply for the license.

Most agents are paid by commission, which means you only get paid when you have completed the process/transaction. Most brokerage companies are anxious to hire new agents because of this 'free' factor. Choose the company carefully, and benefit from some essential training while performing your job duties.

This is why it is essential to consider becoming a part-time agent unless you believe you have a 'nest egg' large enough to cover you until you make your first sale.

Time-Saving Techniques

That first paycheck could be in the distant future, so you have to set a path and begin the journey. Multi-tasking will be normal as the day progresses from team meetings, preparation of marketing packages, lunches with creditors, and showing perspective properties to clients.

You can improve your skills for time management by becoming focused and prioritizing your duties, devising a system that works for your daily tasks, and utilizing all of the tools you can to make the process simpler.

Focus

These are some essential tips to get you headed in the right direction to become more productive and focused:

> **Focus Tip 1: Outline your life and business goals.** It is time for you to decide which specialization you will focus on whether it is investment properties, or areas with no improvements or infrastructure (raw land as it is called in real estate). After that goal set, you can discover ways to improve and do the best possible job.
>
> It is time to decide how much time you will be placing into your real estate position. Do you have a family? How much time will you have available for work? If you're single, you can approach the 24/7 routine, but you still need to set a baseline of how much time you want to dedicate to your new practice.

> **Focus Tip 2: Organize and prioritize your workload.** It is important to have a blueprint for keeping your business functioning successfully. Keep records of your 'comings and goings' for a few days to discover how much you can improve your time management skills. Many tools are available on the Internet free of charge, such as *toggle.com*. If you know how many hours you spend on a particular activity, it is much easier to adjust your schedule.

> **Focus Tip 3: Keep an active to-do list.** If you can remain focused in the important work, it will be much more difficult to get off-track or forget important showings or appointments. You can refer to several programs including *todoist.com* or the *Google Calendar*. Take advantage of the different extension

platforms and apps for web browsers, email, or mobile devices.

➢ **Focus Tip 4: Don't waste time.** Unfortunately, wasted time can cost you money ranging from waiting for conferences to start, being left on hold, or standing in lines. The to-do list will be a monitor to keep you on target during these lost bits of time. Have a strategy for occasions when you know you will be stuck in lingo; grab your phone and get busy.

Make a Plan

After you have the time element covered, it is time to make a system that works for each of your daily tasks. These are a few ways to save some time:

➢ **Time-Blocking:** Special times should be set where no interruptions will invade your time-block. Take this special time for managing your transactions or returning calls to clients. You can reach out to social media during this time for ways to improve your business status. By setting a time for these activities; you won't worry about them during the regular course of the day.

➢ **Batching:** Each daily task can be grouped such as batching your phone calls and emails to be checked at specific times during the day. A lot of time can be wasted if you stop what you a doing to answer immediately. If the call is important, a message will be left on the machine. You will also have a permanent record of the call.

Access the Tools

Many of the 'old-timers' don't believe the Internet is an essential tool. However, with the use of the Internet, you can access free time management apps such as these:

- *Dropbox.com*
- *Evernote.com*
- *MyLifeOrganized.net*
- *RememberTheMilk.com*

In today's fast-paced market, social networking is what this country's foothold to attract the necessary buyers and sellers necessary for the marketing of real estate. At first, search for the deals to get the job done without breaking the bank.

Independence or Franchise

Once you have all of your credentials, you will need to weigh the pros and cons of working for yourself/solo or working with a franchise or chain. These are some of the elements to consider:

Chain and Franchise	Pros	Cons
	Larger Inventory to List	Less Input from You
	Strong Referral Network	Cannot Freely Experiment
	More Formal Training	Higher Initiation Fees
	Stronger Resources	Higher Costs of Operation
	More Technology Advances	Limited Marketing and Branding
Independent Agent		
	Lower Costs as an agent	Less Guidance or Support
	More Flexible	Fewer formal training opportunities
	Local Credibility	Resistant to Amendments or changes
	More input on programs/policies	Fewer resources/Smaller network

Chapter 3:
House Flipping Basics

Before you decide flipping houses is for you; you need to realize you will make some mistakes on the chosen path. However, by fully understanding the process, you can still make a minimal or large profit. As with any other occupation, it takes time to learn all of the 'ropes,' and how to avoid all of the hazards. Experience is the best teacher. First, you need to understand the lingo/terms used including flipping!

Flip it Right: Popularity has gained over the past several years with television coverage of flipping houses for a profit. The process is much more involved than purchasing a home at an auction, making some cosmetic changes, and selling it off to the first bidder.

When you purchase distressed property; you renovate the areas which need repair. You are providing a service that adds real value to the property. You are not only strengthening the emerging house recovery while making a profit; you are providing living spaces for individuals and families.

It's Not a Simple Process: Flipping is a fast paced challenge full of potential risk and a lot of hard work. The traditional process requires cash to purchase and make improvements, meaning you need to realize you need to be aware of what is involved before you cash is on the line.

Flipping for Beginners: Cash Flow

Your first step involves whether you have the cash to begin the flipping process. Do you have enough cash to begin the challenge or will you need to locate investor? If you don't, there are many ways to fund your project using other resources. These are a few of the ways to proceed without investing your money:

Partners: The easiest way to start with no money is to choose a partner who has the funding necessary to head such a task. The candidates can include a co-worker, relative, close friend, business associate, or another real estate investor. You could also include your attorney or anyone in your neighborhood that has a successful business.

For example, you could be responsible for all of the legwork for the investment if you can locate a partner to finance the deal. At the time of the sale, the team would split the profits fifty-fifty. However, some investors like to be solo for a short time to test the waters, and complete one deal at a time. It is your choice!

Private Money Lenders: Approaching private lenders can provide you with the needed money from individuals who have money invested in 401ks, IRAs, mutual funds or have a large chunk of equity in his/her home. These resources can be leveraged for investment in real estate.

Hard Money Lenders (HMLs): This group of financers is generally small groups or private individuals that lend money (via the term hard money) based on the property—not on your credit score. The percentage rates can sometimes be twice that or regular mortgage companies with higher origination fees.

The upside is that you can fund up to 100% of the money needed for the purchase. With the downside; you might need to reinforce the loan with collateral such as with your personal assets. In this situation, you could use the hard money to make some quick fixes to raise the value of the property. At that point, you could receive a new loan from a bank based on the new property value to pay off the hard loan.

Network for Investors: Have your freshly printed cards at hand and mingle with the right people. Make appointments using every resource at your disposal, including the Internet. These are some of the networks to begin your search with using Google:

- Real Estate Investors Association (REIA) at *http://www.nationalreia.com/*

  Search for local meetings in your area.

- Real estate investment meetings could be researched at Meetup: *https://www.meetup.com/*

- Your Business Networking International Chapter

- Your Local Chamber of Commerce

The opportunities will not come to you; you have to search for them. You could also form a local real estate investors association of your own.

Search for Foreclosures

Many times, you can purchase a piece of property listed below its marketing value. You can check with government agencies, banks, auction houses, asset management companies, and many others.

Build a House Flipping Team

Making a profit while flipping property require more than gathering the cash; it requires a process of trial and error to achieve the team that will be on your side. Even if you are experienced, handling a flip isn't a one person job; it takes a team of professionals to accomplish the task. These are some of the areas you must consider:

Hire a Reputable General Contractor: A trustworthy contractor can make or break any deal because he/she will run the project. The contractor will be responsible for hiring all of the subcontractors needed for the flip including electricians, carpenters, and plumbers.

Choose the Real Estate Agent: You should hire someone who has experience when selling flipped houses. It is also possible—if you have the requirements—to train the person you choose for your agent. An agent can also destroy or lose the deal; so choose carefully. Be sure you check the following elements:

- Research the agent's credentials.
- Look at his/her current listings.
- Talk with his/her recent clients.
- Look up his/her licensing to be sure it is current.

Hire an Attorney: Having the assistance of a qualified attorney will benefit you in the long term. Online advice is good for starters, but you need the quality education that can only be provided by the professionals.

Locate a Certified Public Accountant (CPA): Unless you have the qualifications, you need someone who is familiar with the United States tax laws pertaining to real estate investment as well as house flipping. A competent CPA can keep the IRS content and keep your taxes as low as possible.

Hire a Knowledgeable Insurance Agent: The process of flipping homes will require an agent who understands your business and can provide you with good advice. He/ she needs to be aware of the different types of properties you plan on purchasing during the flipping contracts.

Locate the House

Flipping is a challenge, but the suitable property is another huge step. You need to consider the geographic location and research for the lower priced homes as a starting point. You have all of the right elements covered, so use your team to uncover the perfect location. After your team of experts helps you check the property for possible repairs, you make the choice to decline or purchase.

For example, your real estate agent will find the property and your contractor can provide you with an estimate of what he/she believes the job will cost. You also need to have your insurance agent involved in the process. As stated previously, this is not a one person job. Enlist the use of an agent and a real estate wholesaler to assist you with the kind of property you want to flip.

Flip the Math and Supervise

Some of the professionals call the analysis you perform before you flip a house as 'napkin math.' You need to be sure the property has potential before you invest. Simple math lets you know you are searching for the After Repair Value (ARV). If the initial figures look promising; you might have your ideal property project.

However, as you proceed, don't rely 100% on the team because you should oversee the process and watch as the rehab takes place. This is how you know the project is progressing according to the budget as it was set aside at the onset of the flip.

Make the Profit

You profit is determined on how quickly and efficiently your team can remodel the home. The longer it sits in lieu of repair, the longer it will take for you to place it on the market. After all, you cannot get top dollar for a property when the home is torn apart or unlivable.

As with any business, flipping takes teamwork. The professionals set a time limit and strive for that date. With all of the right calculations, many of the companies can flip a home within six months if no unforeseen situations arise during the process.

Chapter 4:
Rental Property Basics

The good part of your incentive to become better informed includes how to procure rental property. You might decide to do a bit of solo searching before you call a real estate agent. The most essential element is taking an unbiased approach at the neighborhoods you may need to consider that are within your investment range.

These are some of the main elements to consider when probing for the perfect property to meet your prerequisites:

Neighborhood

You have to first consider your location and whether you want to have someone else manage the property or if you plan on managing it yourself as the landlord. You need to consider which tenants will be attracted to your property. For example, if you have property close to a beach, you will be swamped with tenants during the summer months and have more vacancies during the winter. You could also have real estate close to a university with similar circumstances.

Future Development

Check with the municipal planning department in the desired area to see is any new zoning is under development. This could bring malls, business parks, and condos. The only problem is that this can hurt the value of adjoining properties. For example, if you have your mind set on a home that has beautiful woodland as a perk; you don't want a shopping mall to be built in its place.

Property Taxes

Consideration must be given concerning how much of the tenant's money you will need to be set aside for taxes. The information is filed in the town's assessment office so you can be prepared for the necessary expense. Taxes are calculated by the area, and living in a neighborhood with higher taxes indicates you have a valuable property.

Crime

Gather statistics of criminal activity from several areas before you make a choice of property investment. The homeowner might not be a good resource. Visit the area at different times of the afternoon, evening, or night, and speak with different neighbors; they will probably give you the true facts.

You want to check for recent activity whether it is slowing down or speeding up for petty crimes. You also need to see if any serious crimes or vandalism rates are frequently reported to the police. After all, who wants to live in a hot crime rated area other than criminals?

Number of Vacancies and Listings

Be aware of red flags such as one specific neighborhood having a remarkably large amount of listings. You need to inspect the possibilities and consider whether it is a seasonal area which could explain the vacant homes. The cycle runs in marketing for lowered vacancy rates provide the opening higher rental rates. Higher vacancy rates can force you (the landlord) to lower rents to keep the units rented.

Average Rental Prices

Investigate and determine what the average rental prices are in the area. This will determine whether the location is the one you want to make a profit. Forecast what the prices can be in the future. For now, the rental might be sufficient to cover expenses such as the taxes and mortgage payments, but you have to look ahead for the big picture. You can use the Internet to see the general prices of rent in your area at *https://www.rentometer.com/*.

Amenities

Start with some research to discover areas under development or established with gyms, movie theaters, halls, gyms, or other activities which will attract potential renters. It is also good to know where the bus stops or train stations are located in the area. Google can be your best friend throughout the search.

If your clients have children, it is good to search for areas where parks, lakes, or amusement parks are located. If the area is good for the family's children, you probably will have a new tenant if the home is suitable.

Job Markets

The United States Bureau of Labor Statistics is a good place to discover how a particular location is rated. Searching for companies that might start construction in a precise area is an excellent spot to acquire rental property. However, you must also deliberate; more people can have an effect of the property values, whether it is positive or negative reactions. As a business person, would you want to live in the area? If the answer is yes, it will most likely be a respectable choice.

Schools

If your renters have children, a good school is essential. You should analyze whether the school is maintained because it can have an effect on your valuable investment. If the area has a bad reputation, you might have difficulties finding worthy tenants. Even though you are concerned about the monthly profits, you need to consider the property's value if you decide to sell it.

Natural Disaster

In relation to insurance, you need to deduct it from your rental returns. You need to consider how much is necessary for your property. As previously mentioned, if you are in a beach area that is at risk for flooding, the insurance will be higher. Any natural disaster can churn away your income if you aren't sufficiently covered for the unexpected losses.

The Perfect Investment

For most beginners, single-family dwellings or a condominium is a superb investment property. Low-maintenance is a plus in a condo because a community association is usually responsible for external repairs. However, since most condos are independent living units; you cannot collect the higher rents that could be received from single-family homes.

Long-term renters—families or couples—tend to be a good choice for single-family real estate opportunities. You want to have a tenant that is qualified as a responsible party, and will pay the rent on time while taking care of the premises.

Check the properties that you can and cannot afford, because many real estate agents will sell below the listing price. Once you have the final selling price, you will have a good general idea of the market value of the home. Search for a property that needs a bit of remodeling to bring in higher rent. You will also have the process underway by raising the property value in case you want to sell it in later years.

Meet the Tenants

If you purchase buildings such as apartments with tenants; discover what type of rental agreements/leases are in effect. You should know how long they have lived in the home. During the spring and summer, tenants tend to move out more frequently versus the winter or fall months.

After you have a listing of the current tenants, you will need to make a marketing plan to advertise the vacancies. Begin with photos of the property inside and out and list them on sites such as *Craigslist, Zillow,* or *Rent.com*.

Run the Numbers

Be sure to do the math! You should begin by taking the area's average rent and deduct your forecasted monthly payment including property taxes and insurance. Divide the two figures by 12 and allow for repairs and general maintenance to the home and property. Set the budget high and leave the money ready available in case of unexpected circumstances.

The projections are one of the most essential steps you will perform during the process of acquiring rental properties. These are some of the elements that can quickly sabotage the rental property and its profitability:

- Extreme Interest Expenditure
- Unanticipated Disasters
- Paying too much for the property
- Maintenance/Upkeep and Utilities
- Insurance Costs
- Excessive Property Taxes
- Home Owner's Association (HOA) Fees

After you consider these factors, proceed carefully to achieve the numbers according to your projections/forecast.

Challenge the Predictions

You have to second-guess you calculations. For example you have decided on $800 for a monthly rent. Is this a reliable calculation for the area? Is the information from an unbiased resource?

Calculations were made using a 15% vacancy rate. Why do you choose that number? Do you have marketing date for proof or actual experience to verify the estimate?

Maintenance and repairs are a must to be figured into a budget. Do you know how to inspect the property for an estimate? Do you know what types of repairs are needed?

It is possible some of your calculations are incorrect. What do you do from that point? Do you cut your losses and sell the property at a lower price or 'bite the bullet' and make the repairs?

The point is to be sure you have the right information by using credible sources at the time of your forecasting. Remember the saying from the *Karate Kid* series, 'wax on and wax off" as you proceed. For example, if the wax is not done correctly, you won't have a shiny car, right? The same is true with real estate, you have to have a good base number to make the correct decisions and produce a property that will become profitable.

Financing and the Purchase Price

Your calculations will depend on how you are closing the deal; whether it will be financed or an all cash deal. You are probably asking why purchase with cash instead of financing. Several reasons have an effect on this conclusion:

- ➢ The investor wanted to generate the cash flow quickly.
- ➢ Ready cash was available.
- ➢ The property was inexpensive.

Advantages of Financing

For every dollar placed into the property from 'out of your pocket,' consider the money working harder than if you cover the full price of the property without financing. That means the cash on cash return is over two times higher than when you use other people's money.

If you finance the package, you will not need to have as much up front money for the property as well as the source of income that comes along with the property. Financing provides you the potential to propagate your real estate portfolio by purchasing quickly and raking in the cash.

Disadvantages of Financing

If you want to avoid debt because of personal reasoning; this approach will not suit your conviction.

The cash flow will be impeded for thirty years and you will be strapped to monthly payments. The property will not cost as much 'up front' but after the payment is made, you will have less cash flow monthly.

Property Taxes

Whether you own the property or have it finance, you will always pay property taxes. To verify this information, go to the City Treasurer's website for your location and search for the annual totals from the past two years or you can check the seller's Schedule E tax form.

Insurance and Utilities

Most insurance companies are a reliable connection to find out how to plan for insuring the property. Many rental properties furnish the water, but the remainder of the utilities is paid by the current tenant.

Property Management and Maintenance

Most property managers receive a minimum of ten percent of the gross rental revenue for his/her services. If you decide to manage the property, this will be your profit. Another ten percent of the gross revenue is set aside for repairs and maintenance. You might go some time without any issues—let the money accumulate—in case of an unforeseen situation or emergency.

Chapter 5:
REIT Basics

Real Estate Investment Trust or REIT is an enterprise which finances or owns real estate that produces income. REITs were created by Congress in 1960 in a larger scale to produce accessible real estate to average investors. This process works similar to the way anyone invests in other industries—from the purchases of equity. REIT's qualifications require that of its taxable income, (90%) must be distributed to its shareholders in the usage of dividends.

REIT's stockholders earn benefits derived (pro-rated) from income produced by commercial real estate ownership. REITs can offer reliable dividends portfolio diversification, liquidity, transparency, and firm long-term performance.

Types of REITs

Don't be confused because a REIT is not a partnership but a vertically integrated company. REIT profiles with two main categories:

Mortgage REITS

Money is generally lent directly to the real estate operators and owners, or the organization will provide an extension of credit with the use of mortgage-backed securities or the acquisition of loans. Some of the strategies used include dynamic hedging techniques or securitized mortgage investments, and other acceptable derivative means. This is the best way to handle credit risks and still manage the interest rates.

Equity REITs

A REIT has to obtain and improve its properties predominantly as part of its portfolio versus reselling them once development is completed. They mostly operate and own a widespread range of real estate dealings such as improvement of real property and resident services, leasing, as well as maintaining them. Approximately 10% of REITS are mortgaged and the other 90% is equity.

Properties Owned and Managed by REITs

A variety of properties are incorporated with REIT including office buildings, warehouses, healthcare facilities, shopping centers, hotels, and many others. Specializations usually have one type of facility such as self-storage facilities, shopping malls, data centers, or in some areas timberlands.

Financial Benefits of REIT

Benefits of REIT			
Diversification	Increases Return by Reducing Risk	Finalizes Asset Distribution	Low Correlation with Broader Market
Income	Reduce Portfolio Instability	Steadfast income Returns	Wealth and Dividends Accumulation
Inflation Protection	Accepted Inflation Hedge	Returns Steadily Outperform Consumer Price Index (CPI)	Low and High Inflation
Performance	Improved returns vs. Corporate Bonds	Deliver Income & Growth	Outperformed S&P Index over most periods
Liquidity	Strategic Asset Allocation	Portfolio Restored	Purchased and sold similar to other equities
Transparency	Market Transparency	Resilient Corporate Authority	Tax Transparency

Disadvantages of REITS

Issue #1

Property taxes must be paid which can total up to 25% of the overall operational expenses. Property taxes could be increased by State and municipal authorities to make up for dropping cash flows to its shareholders or to make up for deficits in the budget.

Issue #2

REITs are sensitive to demand for other high-yield assets which could make Treasury securities more attractive. This could lower their share prices and draw funds away from REITs.

Issue #3

Tax rates are generally fifteen percent higher because of the high yields. This is due to the fact that about three-quarters of its dividends are considered ordinary income.

How to Form a REIT

Draft a partnership agreement designating the percentage of ownership as well as the responsibilities of each partner. There must be a minimum of one hundred investors after the first year of operation to quality for REIT.

The Secretary of State will incorporate your management company in the state of operation. One condition of REIT is that is must begin as a limited liability corporation (LLC).

A board of trustees or directors is the managers that must invest at least three-quarters of its overall assets in real estate. A minimum of 95% of the gross income must be from those investments.

Draft the Private Placement Memorandum (PPM) listing the principals of the corporation, its strategies, and the properties that REIT plans to invest.

Amend your Certificate of Incorporation after the 100 investors have committed. You need to file the certificate with the Secretary of State's office. Once completed, you will be recognized as a REIT, which eliminates tax payments for the corporation.

The final step is to file Form 1120 to the IRS. By maintaining the 90% pay outs of earnings, you will REIT status and tax benefits.

Chapter 6:
Property Wholesaling Basics

If you have some determination and a bit of specialized knowledge; you can build income with just minimal credit and capital. You don't need a real estate license because you will have reasonable/equitable interest in the piece of property. The interest can be from a contract (property is under a contract) or you have the title or own the property.

Cash, hard money loans, or lines of credit are used by an investor to purchase property listed by a wholesaler. The properties are usually distressed and need extensive repairs which will lead to a quick closing. A wholesaler is a hard hitter because the focus is placed on two items: networking and finding super deals (no matter what the damages to the property). He/she is there to make a fast buck, and is considered as a middle man/woman.

Basic Steps for a Real Estate Wholesaler

1) Make the Offer.

2) Upon Acceptance of the offer; sign the contract to purchase.

3) Begin the Title Work.

4) Start the marketing process to locate a buyer.

5) Reach an acceptable agreement with the prospective owner/buyer.

6) Qualify the potential purchaser.

7) Sign the contract with the buyer and collect the deposit.

8) Submit the paperwork to the title company.

9) Attend the settlement.

It is as simple as that but it takes proper understanding to make sure you have a successful business arrangement.

Determine the Amount to Offer

The most daunting element for a beginner wholesaler is calculation the offer for a desired property. The professionals suggest these steps to make the decision:

Step 1: Choose a farming/rural area and discover who the active investors are for that parcel. This is an essential part of the plan of wholesaling property.

Step 2: Once you have located the investors, discuss with them with what other deals he/she might be seeking. You could inquire for the square footage needed the type of construction, price range, and similar questions. The main point is to get your name out there. Give him/her a card and consider more of the investors. This is how you find out what prices individuals are willing to pay for segments of property in that area.

Step 3: If the plan is successful you should have several of the active buyers in the farming area. You then seek the MLS and begin to make offers for properties which will fit the criteria described by the buyers. You must make sure to leave some 'wiggle room' for yourself and your end purchaser.

Using this three step plan will ensure you that you are investing in property that is currently in demand; making your return on investment (ROI) quickly.

Deals Gone South

So far, you have had the perfect plan with several lists of perspective clients for the property you have just acquired. However, the entire list failed, and you need to act quickly. These are some of the things you can do to move the investment:

Contact Local Landlords: Survey the area of all of the real estate that is for rent, and contact the agent. See if any of them are interested in obtaining your package.

Anchor Signs on the Property: Other investors may also see your sign while he/she is out for a drive. Check the local area's code enforcement in case the signs are not allowed. This is a free way to advertise, and will almost always guarantee some activity from them.

Visit the County Website: Go to the county's section 8 website to gain a list of the landlords for the other properties in your zone. Also, research the property appraiser website for active investors in the area. Simply use Google, and your county, along with any information you have on the property.

Disadvantages of Wholesaling: The investment market is unpredictable. Some of the properties might take months or longer to resell, but some will close quickly.

Assigning a Contract

You can sign a purchase agreement and sell it to another investor to purchase downright—which makes you the middle person in the deal. The job is similar to a real estate agent whereas you had a signed purchase agreement between the seller and yourself—giving you equitable interest.

Wholesaling is an asset on paper which can be sold to a third party for an assignment fee. It is like you never owned the property. Along with a contract comes another list of questions. Do you know what kind of Assignment Agreement needs signing? What kind of Purchase Agreement do you need? Do you know when you will receive your money? How do you close the deal?

In a 'Nut Shell'

Investor/Buyer A locates a deal and signs the Purchase Agreement with the Seller who has the option to sell/assign the paper to another Investor/Buyer B.

An Assignment Agreement is used when Buyer A assigns/sells the Purchase Agreement to Buyer B. This transfers the rights from Buyer/Investor A from any obligation or liability.

The process is smooth which shows up on the records as a purchase from the seller, at the same terms, price, deadlines, and other information from the original document.

Let the Seller Be Aware

Since you will be operating as a wholesaler, you should be sure the seller is aware of the following:

- ➤ You are not purchasing the property.
- ➤ You are selling the contract to another person, and they will purchase the property.
- ➤ The seller will stay informed during the process.
- ➤ If a buyer isn't located, the contract will expire since there was no transaction.

Compile the Property Prospectus Report

It is relevant for you to know the general information about the property and home that you have under contract. You will be using a buyers list which you have compiled of potential cash buyers. You need to cover items such as these:

- ➤ Listing Price
- ➤ Property Address
- ➤ The Parcel Number
- ➤ Legal description of the property
- ➤ Size of the Property
- ➤ The Terrain and Surroundings
- ➤ Road and Utility Access
- ➤ Parcel Map

- On-Site Photos

- Cost Breakdowns

Diagnose the Serious Calls

You need to weed through the endless line of 'busy-bodies' who are just being curious. You can relay these steps to them as a pattern breaker. The serious will respond to the questions such as these:

- Ask to have the Assignment Agreement signed and returned by email or fax to 6 pm that day.

- Ask that he/she sends you the money for a deposit by 6 pm that day using a wire transfer service.

The interested party must understand the property will not be held until these two items are completed. It is a 'first-come—first served' kind of situation.

Joint Ventures in Wholesaling

Whether newly established or not, joining other wholesalers are advantageous for many reasons. These are a few:

- Use another wholesaler's inventory to use in your buyer's listing.

- Establish a larger buyer baseline.

- As a beginner, you can tap into an active buyer's listing.

One of the biggest advantages is that if the property is sold, a standard agreement is usually a 50/50 proposition. You will enter into a co-wholesaling agreement that will specify your benefits including the terms, compensation, and a compete/non-circumvention clause to protect the interest of the wholesaler in the property. Do some research and use the following information:

- Bandit signs will help you locate those who are active in the buyer seller market.

- Internet sites including *Backpage* or *Craigslist*, or 'for sale by owner' sites.'

- Check the Internet for the wholesaler in your city using Google

This is one of the areas a beginner can benefit when first entering the real estate platform. Eventually, you would like to be on your own, but you first need to build your inventory and learn the ropes. You can earn enough money during the process to take your business to the next level. However, you have to consider you will be splitting the profits at the same time.

Chapter 7:
What Buyers Expect from a Realtor

Some expectations are forefront with buyers in relation to what is expected from a realtor. It won't matter which type of property you have available, but if you know what the buyer needs, you can be prepared to get the most out of the time spent with the prospective client.

Trustworthiness

An agent must tell the client the truth, even if it causes the sale to be lost. It is okay to boast of the many great items the home or property has to offer, but the defects should also be mentioned so the buyer doesn't change his/her mind later on when it is time to do a final walk-thru at closing. This honest approach could also let the buyer know you are on his/her side and do not want to take advantage of the situation.

Quick Response Time

It is essential to respond to any emails, calls, or texts as soon as possible. You might lose a sale if he/she is searching for an agent.

Methods of Communication

It is advisable to ask the prospective buyer which method of communication is acceptable. Some clients prefer texting, whereas others prefer a phone call or email for relaying messages.

Provide Intelligent Content

As a real estate agent/investor you need to let the customer know you have the experience and education required to place him/her in the home of his/her dreams. You have to stay in demand by reading all of the relevant or current information in the real estate industry. Updating your education through training seminars can also let your customers know you are there and know what he/she is experiencing.

Use your most professional yet friendly approach with your clients. Most buyers appreciate the friendly vibe. The most useful insight you can have is to be prepared. Know the answers to the questions before the buyer has a chance to ask them. Let your buyers know you are there for their needs, and you will have the word-of-mouth advertising you have been seeking.

Conclusion

Thank for making it through to the end of *Real Estate: Going From Novice to Full-Time Real Estate Pro*, let's hope it was enlightening and effective to providing you with all of the tools you need to achieve your goals whatever it may be.

The subsequent step is to make the ultimate choice concerning what you plan on doing with your future investments. You now have the knowledge necessary to move forward whether you decide to become an agent or remain in the industry as an investor, you have the implements.

Many of the professionals believe there is no 'right' time to invest in the real estate market. If you start out modestly with just a few property locations, you will begin to appreciate and see the capital grow until it is time to begin your next endeavor.

That doesn't mean you have to continue to purchase low-end properties; you can move on with the knowledge you now have to improve your future. The larger the investment, the quicker the assets will appreciate. However, the larger properties are superb for comparison to the smaller ones in your possession as a portfolio.

If you are considering the stock market, the real estate market is similar, but in real estate, when the market crashes; you still have tangible assets which can be recouped. Be realistic, even though many others have failed to become successful in the real estate market; many of the problems could be related to a poor business plan.

Once you have established some authority in your field, you can focus on a targeted population. But for now, you have the right tools to get started!

As a final point, if you found this book valuable, a personal appraisal on Amazon is cordially appreciated! Thank you.

www.ingramcontent.com/pod-product-compliance
Lightning Source LLC
Chambersburg PA
CBHW061225180526
45170CB00003B/1157